From Reviews for *Succeeding in High School*

**A solid and recommended read for any who
wants to use high school as a launch pad for life**

"High School is where it really starts to matter, "Succeeding in High School: A Handbook for Teens and Parents plus a College Admissions Primer" is a guide for young adults who want to make the most out of their college education and better prepare themselves for college and the rest of their lives. From making the most out of the first year to the importance of extracurriculars, there is no shortage of wisdom and advice within. "Succeeding in High School" is a solid and recommended read for any who wants to use high school as a launch pad for life."

-*Midwest Book Review*

The importance of good information
and thoughtful advice

"I found this book easy to read and while it is specifically written in relation to the American education system, much of the advice provided and suggestions made would be useful to students (and their parents) in other countries. While the book is aimed primarily at high school students, I think it would also be useful (at least for parents) of younger children.

Mr. Adegboyega-Edun is an educator who clearly has drawn on his experience (of over 20 years) in preparing and presenting this book. Each chapter begins with a student quote, and ends with `Questions for Students', `Things to Do' and `For Parents'. This serves to both reinforce the points made as well as to make it clear that effective learning requires action by both students and their parents or carers."

-J. Cameron-Smith "Expect the Unexpected"
- Amazon.com Top 500 Reviewer

Some really great information.....
NOT just for high school students

"This is an excellent book but I think it should be for pre-teen and even younger students' parents because waiting until high school to get serious about your education can often be too late for many. In the book the author discusses laying a strong academic foundation in ninth grade, developing good organizational skills, study habits, selecting courses that fit college bound plans, how to handle stress, extracurricular activities, knowing what the graduation requirements are, early graduation, some myths about homework, challenging yourself, diversifying your college or university search. And much more."

-MotherLodeBeth "MotherLodeBeth"

-Amazon.com Top 100 Reviewer

Succeeding in High School Reviewed
By Wendy Thomas of Bookpleasures.com

"*Succeeding in High School* is a handbook for teens and parents on how to stay the course in the often confusing halls of high school. . . .

Each chapter thoroughly explains a skill using plenty of examples and then concludes with questions for the students to get them thinking about how they can accomplish specific goals, things to do which are action items for students, and a parents' section filled with tips and advice to support their students in school.

Using clear language that never talks down to the reader, *Succeeding in High School* does a great job of sorting out what needs to be done by the students and their parents in order for kids to successfully complete high school and then move on to college."

-Wendy Thomas, BookPleasures.com

New "Handbook" aims to guide students to success

"High school can be tough — from the anxiety of social situations to the pressures of college applications, many students find themselves overwhelmed by stress.

Joseph Adegboyega-Edun is a high school counselor who is determined to help students succeed — both emotionally and academically — in the four most important and challenging years of their K12 education. . . .

This guide also lets parents know how to advocate for their teen's education and how to keep track of their teen's progress.

For those who are college-bound, *Succeeding in High School* uses a step-by-step approach to mastering the college application process, from organizing the search, finding the right college, filling out the applications and obtaining financial aid."

-Staff Report, myCentralJersey.com,
A GANNETT COMPANY

A Clear Plan to College

"Adegboyega-Edun writes in a well organized fashion which makes it easy to understand. This is a great resource for students and parents that are unfamiliar with navigating the college admission process. It will also help students formulate goals for their future while they are still in high school. As a community college professor, I see students and parents everyday still wondering why they didn't do things earlier. I will recommend this book to everyone with students in high school as many of their fears and questions will be answered in less than 140 pages."

-Professor M. Bruner, Deltareviewer
Reviewing for Real Page Turners

Succeeding in High School

Succeeding in High School

A Handbook
for Teens and
Parents *plus*
A College
Admissions
Primer

Joseph Adegboyega-Edun

America's Counselor
Frederick, Maryland

Succeeding in High School
A Handbook for Teens and Parents plus A College Admissions Primer
All Rights Reserved.
Copyright © 2011 Joseph Adegboyega-Edun
v4.0

Cover Photo © 2011 America's Counselor. All rights reserved.

America's Counselor
www.americascounselor.com

America's Counselor, the 9, 12, steps and pyramid logo, and the 9-12 golden graduation scroll are trademarks of America's Counselor.

ISBN: 978-0-578-08846-4

PRINTED IN THE UNITED STATES OF AMERICA

To Moyo, for her encouragement,
support, and patience over the years.

CONTENTS

CHAPTER 3 33
ABOUT YOU, YOUR HOME, AND STRESS: COPING WHEN TIMES ARE TOUGH AND REDUCING DISTRACTIONS

CHAPTER 4 47
EXTRACURRICULAR ACTIVITIES

CHAPTER 5 55
SUCCESSFUL STUDY STRATEGIES

ACKNOWLEDGMENTS

Thanks to the admission officers of several colleges and universities, including the following: Brown University, Cabrini College, College of Charleston, James Madison University, Towson University, University of South Carolina, University of Virginia and Vanderbilt University.

HIGH SCHOOL, IN BRIEF

This book is about how students of various academic levels of achievement can help themselves, and how parents, teachers and other adults can help them be successful in high school. While each student's post-high school plan may be different, the single most important credential needed to pursue this goal is still the high school diploma.

U.S. Department of Education statistics indicate that about half of freshmen drop out of two-year colleges while about one quarter of freshmen drop out of four-year colleges. If students consider the projection that four out of five jobs will require some form of post-secondary education, they'll see that it's important to take their high school education seriously.

High school is tough, as students find out in the first two to three weeks of their freshman year. There will be times when they experience great stress because they have little time to complete so many of the assignments they're getting in nearly every subject area. Such assignments must be duly completed and turned in on time to avoid poor grades.

Some students will wonder why they should take courses they don't like and which may not be relevant to their future plans just because these courses are "requirements for graduation." At some point in their high school careers, some students will experience conflicts with close friends at school, fall sick, or sustain an injury during sports.

When they feel down and in distress, students need to think of what they can do to make high school easier for them. Getting involved in some activity that they enjoy or finding something new to learn and do will help. So will looking for exciting non-academic things to do that will enrich their experiences.

The requirements for a high school diploma keep changing as curricula are expanded and rigorous exit tests are added to ensure that high school graduates can compete successfully with their counterparts throughout the world.

It is reasonable to assume that upon graduating high school, some students plan to attend four-year colleges of varying levels of selectivity while others plan to attend their local community colleges. Yet others may opt for military training and there will be some who will work after they graduate. Each group will need a high school diploma.

Making sure that they get all the help they need from home and from school staff is likely to make their journey through high school less difficult.

For Parents

Parents and guardians of high school students often want to know how they can help their high school teens in the best possible way. The four years of high school form the most difficult part of a student's K-12 education. As their teens enter the freshman year of high school, parents and guardians find that their teens' grades, attendance and relationships with friends and teachers now matter in a way that they had not been before. One missed day of school now means several hours of work to be made up. Two or more missed days may need more drastic steps to ensure that the student does not get too far behind. One bad grade on a test in any subject now becomes a matter for concern. This is because the high school academic record or transcript is a permanent record. This means that every final grade in every subject and in every semester follows the student for life. Bad grades hurt. Good grades help.

While for some students a mix of poor grades and good grades in a marking period may be an indication of a valiant struggle to pull through a period of adversity, a collection of poor grades for other students may be a result of not taking high school seriously enough or a mistaken feeling that they can perform last minute wonders with their final exams.

Parents may, and can intervene to help their teens perform better by monitoring grades, establishing a relationship with teachers, and encouraging the student to make use of free tutoring help at school. This book shows parents what to do, when to do it, and how to do it. It helps parents to identify and make use of opportunities which may be available at their teens' high school. It shows parents and guardians how to spot a problem before it becomes an impediment to their teens' education.

The support students get at home affects their success in school. This book is an effort to make it as simple as possible for parents and guardians of high school teens to help their students adjust properly and do well in high school.

For Students

This book offers you guidelines so you can have a high school experience that you can remember happily several years after it is over. The main issues that will affect your high school life are your home environment, the courses you take in high school, your relationships with your teachers and your school counselor, and your relationship with your friends. Each of these factors may become the most important of all at various times during your high school career. All will contribute in significant ways to your success in high school.

You may be certain that your four years of high school will be the most important years of your education since kindergarten. High school is where you begin to plan what you are going to do with your life. It is where you have the opportunities to apply for internships and to explore postsecondary options. You may form friendships in high school that may last a lifetime and take part in extracurricular activities that you may continue elsewhere after you graduate.

But high school also means work and lots of it. There are homework assignments, labs and projects which you must submit on due dates. There are tests which you must take and pass. Your first test is how you adjust to high school from middle school. Whether you come into your freshman year from a private school or one of the area middle schools, you still need to pass the adjustment test. It is a test of how you will cope with a different but tougher academic environment.

High school calls on you to take charge of your education and to know when and how to ask for help from your teachers, your school counselor and your parent. It asks you to speak up. This will be easier for some and harder for others. In the four years of high school you will need a number of skills to be successful. This book shows you how to develop and use these skills.

PART ONE
HIGH SCHOOL

CHAPTER 1
CROSSING THE BRIDGE: FROM MIDDLE SCHOOL TO HIGH SCHOOL

I thought ninth grade would be like last year. I was wrong. The teachers gave us homework like crazy and some of the work took me hours to do each night. They gave lots of quizzes and tests. I did the work but barely had time for anything else. That wasn't all. Changes in the behavior of kids I used to be friends with, classes moving too fast. Too many kids. Too much homework. —A high school freshman.

In middle school, you did your homework, prepared for tests and did some labs and class assignments. You had lots of time to play and to talk to your friends on the phone. You had time for sports and extracurricular activities. That was then.

You find in high school that there is so much work. You have a homework assignment nearly every day plus lab reports and demanding class assignments involving a lot of writing and problem-solving. If you are in several honors classes, you may find all the work overwhelming. It's going to feel like all you ever have time for is school work, and more school work. If you miss school for two or more days, it seems like you're never going to be able to catch up.

One way to address this high school freshman's frustration is to say that you can only learn what high school involves by experiencing it. But that's not a complete answer because students and parents can learn about high school before the student starts attending. Checking out what information the school has on its website and attending orientation programs help but not totally.

Larger School, Newer Environment

High school means an end to advantages like attending a smaller school, getting to know all your teachers and counselors very quickly and getting good grades easily. Transferring from your middle school to a huge school with more than twice the number of students is a challenging situation. You may not know anyone from your middle school in any of your classes. Because it is difficult to find your friends even at lunchtime, you may lose contact with them eventually. Sometimes, these friends may be in a couple of your classes, but they may find other friends and no longer notice that you are in the same class with them. When this happens, you'll need to find other friends. One way to find new friends is through extracurricular activities.

Your high school classes will move very quickly. Whether you have four, six or seven classes a day, each will seem to fly by. It means you have to pay attention nearly all of the time. It means you have to note what you don't understand so you can ask the teacher. It means you may have to arrange to see the teacher at lunch or after school when you don't understand something.

You can count on a daily assignment in almost all of your high school classes. That's one reason why some high schools give you a planning book or include it in your list of supplies. In a short time, say two weeks or so, you'll find that not doing your homework can be costly, even if you figure a teacher doesn't check it. That's because you will hate your grades. Hating your grades can make you think that school is frustrating. But if you know how you got those grades, you'll know what to do to change them. If you're not sure, start with the teacher. If any of your classes is not working well, see your counselor.

Be quick to find out what additional help your high school offers its students. If there is after school tutoring, find out what the schedule is like, and whether a school bus will be available or a parent has to pick you up when it's over.

As a high school freshman, you are in a unique position because you can make your experience what you want it to be, with some help from your parents and school staff. You want a decent report card every quarter and a good transcript every semester and you start building these from the ninth grade. You don't have to be perfect though no one can stop you from trying to be perfect. At the very least, you want to be sure that you are doing your best, and if certain adults can show you how to get the best results from doing your best, let them.

QUESTIONS FOR STUDENTS

- How much time do you spend on school work after school?
- What activities do you use your home computer for?
- How much time do you spend on each activity?
- How do you use your time when you get less homework?

THINGS TO DO

- On a sheet of paper, list three reasons why you feel it's important for you to succeed in high school.
- List three things you expect to gain from attending high school.
- List three things you will readily do to succeed in high school.
- List three things you expect of your teachers.

FOR PARENTS

- How often do you monitor your high school teen's grades?
- How do you react when your student says, "I have no homework," or "I finished my homework in school"?
- How much time does your teen spend watching TV and/ or use his computer for non-educational activities?
- How do you help your teen manage his time?

CHAPTER 2
CHOOSING YOUR CLASSES:
CHALLENGE YOURSELF
BUT BE CAUTIOUS

I signed up for Honors Algebra 2 because I thought I could do it. Math was never my fun class. It was very hard and I was failing. My math teacher called me after class one day and said he thought I would do better in on-level Algebra 2. I told my parents. I did better in the new class and finished the semester with a B. Two of my friends who stayed in Honors Algebra 2 were not so lucky. One failed. The other passed with a D. —A high school junior

How you choose your classes every year of your high school career may determine whether you will be happy, miserable or somewhere in-between in your core classes, namely English, math, history and science.

While you've heard from your parents, teachers and others that the more honors and advanced classes you take in high school, the better, it need not be too difficult for you to pin down subjects in which you are strong and those in which you are weak. If you are not sure, start with the more challenging level but don't wait too long if you are doing your best and getting help but it's not working out and you risk failing. Some students want to keep trying, even if they're barely passing so it doesn't look as if they're giving up too soon. The longer you remain in a class that's wrong for you, the more frustrated you'll get.

If a class/course isn't working out, tell your parents and your counselor to be sure you replace it with another worthwhile course. Don't wait until it's too late. In some cases, it's better to drop within a week. An example: If your school is on block scheduling, ninety minutes per course and four courses a day, you'll have seven and one-half hours of work to make up if you pick up a new course after a week. Wait two weeks and you have fifteen hours. Each school district sets a deadline to drop courses without penalty, just like colleges. Observe the deadline strictly. Should you drop a course after the deadline, your drop date and withdrawal grade will appear on your transcript.

There are many reasons a high school

student may want to take a class that doesn't fit. A common reason is to be with friends who are in rigorous classes. Another reason is because that's what the parents want and they will pay for tutors if need be. A third reason is to try and see if he can handle the class.

Teachers almost always make course choices easy for high school students. Because they have seen students' performance in their classes, they know students' work habits and can often say if a particular student is better off in an advanced class or in a class that's on-level. Of course, a student may go against such placement, choose an honors or advanced class, do the work in that class and be very successful. It becomes troublesome for the student who goes against the placement and cannot manage the difficult course. What students and parents need to know is that the student's strengths may be in English and history, for example, but not in math and science or vice versa. Students who are thorough when selecting courses, who talk to their teachers and consult their counselors are likely to choose the right courses and be pleased with the academic part of their high school experience.

Know the Graduation Requirements

As you select courses, be aware of what you need to graduate. Check your school and school district's bulletin and check with your counselor if you are new to the school district. Review these requirements every year, crossing out what you've completed. Find out the specific details of your school's graduation requirements. For example, if your school requires four years/ four credits of math but makes algebra and geometry mandatory, take these mandatory math classes and two others. You may take more than the required credits, of course. If biology and one year of physical science are needed but four years of science are required on the whole, work toward meeting these conditions. If exit exams are required, take and pass them. If community service hours are required, work them. Remember that you will only graduate if you meet all of your school's graduation requirements.

Never assume that you can substitute one course credit for a different course credit. For example, do not assume that you can substitute one year of theater for one required credit of English or that one year of art meets the requirement for one credit of physical education. You may wonder why anyone would think this way but students do. If you're not sure of any graduation requirement, consult your counselor so you know what you need. Again, a school will not recommend you for graduation unless you meet all of its graduation requirements. Failing a graduation requirement and not making arrangements to retake it, intercepting interim reports and graduation requirement statements from your school to fool your parents so you can claim later that you did not know that you failed a core class will only delay your graduation date.

Once you know your school's graduation requirements, see if it offers special courses or programs that are of interest to you. If you're passionate about computer-related studies, see what your school has and sign-up if it suits your needs. It is by knowing what your school has to offer that you can use such opportunities to the fullest. Students who are interested in the trades or in career preparatory programs may need to travel daily from their school to a career preparatory center where they spend about one-half of a day in training.

In general, most graduation requirements include four years of English, three
or four years of mathematics to include geometry and algebra, three or four years of
social studies to include civics (government)
and U.S. History, three or four years of science to include physical science and biology,
one year of computer science or technology,
one year of physical education, one year or
one-half year of health education and one
year or two years of a foreign language or an
alternative program like a career preparation
program.

While graduation requirements may not
necessarily state that you must earn a certain grade in a certain course, nothing should
stop you from trying to earn an A in every
class. If you choose your classes well and tai-
lor each to a level you can handle and not
just a level that is most likely to get you an
easy A, you are likely to be successful.

You will also need to be familiar with your
school's method of weighing grades for honors, AP and International Baccalaureate (IB)
classes.

Calculating Grade Point Average

To calculate your Grade Point Average (GPA) for on-level courses, a grade of A=4 Quality Points, B=3 Quality Points, C=2 Quality Points and D=1 Quality Point. If a student gets an A in English I and geometry, a B in social studies, science, and Russian 1 and a C in physical education, you can calculate his GPA as follows if he took each course for one semester and earned 1 (one) credit in each:

English I (A): 1x4=4 Quality Points
Geometry (A): 1x4=4 Quality Points
Social Studies (B): 1x3= 3 Quality Points
Science (B): 1x3=3 Quality Points
Russian 1(B): 1x3=3 Quality Points
Physical Education (C): 1x2=2 Quality Points
Total Quality Points=4+4+3+3+3+2=19
GPA=Quality Points/Number of credits
GPA=19/6=3.16
The student's GPA is 3.16

Selective Colleges and Course Selections

The formula used to weigh grades for honors, AP and IB courses vary from school district to school district and may be different for public and private schools. College admission officers at certain colleges and universities may reconstitute GPA by using the formula above for the core courses only, namely English, math, science, social studies and foreign language. This helps them bring all applicants' GPA to the same level.

Students who plan to apply to selective colleges should know that meeting their school's graduation requirements will not necessarily guarantee their admission. Graduation requirements, like some of the requirements that colleges often state that they expect students to have completed before their high school graduation, are minimum requirements only. Selective colleges check applicants' transcripts against the number of honors and AP courses that their high schools offer, so take courses in subjects you enjoy at the honors and/or AP level. You won't necessarily find them easy but they will help prepare you for whatever your plan after high school may be.

Transfer Students

Being a transfer student means you've come to your high school from another county, another state or another country. It means you need to prepare to adjust to a school system with different policies, procedures and graduation requirements.

School officials who evaluate your transcripts ensure that you are credited with the courses and levels at which you took them from your previous district. From the day you enroll, you are subject to your new school's graduation requirements, which may include passing an exit exam attesting to your proficiency in identified subject areas and a specified number of hours of community service. Ask your counselor about these, even if you are not certain that your family will stay in your new school long enough for you to graduate.

Students transferring from private schools will also need to know what they need to do to graduate from their new high school. In addition, these students need to know that they may not get credit for single trimester courses for which they earned one-third of a credit at their private school because they need to have taken such courses for two trimesters to earn transferable credit. All transferring students should verify that their transcripts indicate the level of the courses they took before they transferred. For example, a receiving school will not give credit for an honors course unless the transcript says so. Credit that counts is not given for courses transferred with Pass/Fail grades and because of this such courses will not count toward graduation at your new school.

As a transfer student, unless you already have a friend at your new school, you'll be facing a difficult transition period. Your classmates may not even notice you for the first few days. Or, they may notice and just ignore you. Being new, you may not know where to start. But saying "Hi" to the kid next to you may start a friendship. On the other hand, it may not, and may leave you wondering why you bothered. You may find clusters of friends gathering together and you feel left out. If you find yourself wondering if coming to this school is a smart thing, you should talk to your counselor.

Some schools have students trained to welcome and support new students like you until such students settle in and find other friends. Members of such an organization might contact you shortly after your enrollment once they receive information about you. Ask your counselor if your school has such an organization.

Participation in extracurricular activities also enables you to meet people with similar interests. If you like athletics, you may become part of a school team. Soon, you'll know so many people that you'll love the school. In every high school, there are several extracurricular activities and you need to start with the one that you care the most about, especially if your reason is to meet people with your type of interests. The school's website, its main office or its counseling office may have information on extracurricular activities.

Your successful social and emotional adjustment to high school will help pave the way to academic success.

International Students

As an international student, you need to know that even if you are transferring to a high school in the United States from an English speaking country, your transcript is still subject to evaluation and you should expect to take placement tests in specific subject areas. If you are from a non-English speaking country, your placement tests are likely to include one to determine appropriate placement in English or in an English Language Learners' (ELL) class.

Specialists use syllabus/curriculum information, the number of clock hours per week a particular class meets each semester or each year, to determine the number of credits a high school course taken in another country should be awarded. A placement test, where applicable, helps to determine the level at which you will now continue your education. It is important to note that sometimes a placement test does not correctly reflect what you know. Consider for example a placement test in mathematics with several word problems. You know the principles and formulas but solving each problem means you must first translate the question. An incorrect translation from English to your original language can get you a low score on the test, leaving you at a lower level of math than your true math skills would show had you continued your education in your home country. As your English language skills improve, you can ask to be moved to a higher level of math.

If some of your subject teachers find that your placements in their classes are not right, they can request a correction on your behalf. There are times when problems arise in a course because it is fast-paced and your mastery of English does not match the speed of the class. Your experience in this case is not unique because it is one reason why some international students who are otherwise well accomplished in math and the sciences find themselves struggling during their first few weeks of high school here. As your knowledge of the English language gets better, your performance in your academic classes will also improve. Ask your English teacher to recommend some books that can help you.

Since two quarters make one semester, if you arrive, say, during the last quarter of any semester, you cannot earn any credit for that semester. This reduces your opportunity to earn high school credit by one semester or one-half of a year. Enrolling at that time and choosing to start immediately means that you will be expected to attend all your classes and do the work anyway although you may be excused from the final exams depending on your school district's policy. This can mean that you are likely to take longer to graduate, so you and your parents should plan accordingly.

Certain core requirements can only be taken at a U.S. high school, for example, U.S. History and U.S Government. Social studies or history courses taken abroad cannot be substituted for these. Exceptions are identical courses taken at American schools abroad. It is worth emphasizing that all students, including international students, must meet graduation requirements in the school district and state where they enroll. Officials will give equivalent credit for each high school subject you took while abroad. If passing state-mandated tests in specific subjects is part of the graduation requirements, such tests are waived in those subjects if you had already earned credit for them in your country.

If community service hours are required, find out how many you need.

You have an opportunity to enroll in an

advanced placement (AP) course if you test into it at a fall semester enrollment. If this is your first exposure to an AP course, it will encourage you to consider advanced placement courses in other subject areas when you feel ready for them.

While the above are key factors that affect your high school education as an international student, another matter arises if you and your family have a very short time to stay here and you know that you cannot meet graduation requirements in that time period. Your parents want you to take only those classes which you will need for graduation in your home country even if such classes do not count toward graduation requirements in this country. You need to be aware that if your parents' plan changes and they are staying for a longer period, you will have to take all courses that count toward graduation requirements here.

Your family circumstances may demand that you leave the United States a couple of weeks before the end of a semester. You worry about not getting credit if you leave without taking final exams. Since a final examination is required in most classes, your school can work with you on alternative ways to test your mastery of each subject so you can earn credit for them.

If you plan to attend college in the U.S. after your high school career, prepare by taking the most demanding courses for which you have prerequisites. You need to ask for and use every opportunity your school provides to help you through the college application process. While you prepare for and take college entrance tests like the SAT and ACT, if you are in an English Language Learners' (ELL) class, consider taking the Test Of English as a Foreign Language (TOEFL) administered by the Educational Testing Service (ETS). You can take the TOEFL in addition to the SAT and/or the ACT.

Homeschooled Students

If you decide to transfer from your homeschooling program to your local high school to continue your education, you are expected to be familiar with the graduation requirements as stated by your supervising school district and your state. If you are transferring to the high school in your attendance area, the transition is likely to be smooth since you know the curriculum. If you move with your family to another state or school district you will need to adjust to differences in curricula and graduation requirements. The new district will evaluate your prior academic record for proper placement. You may take placement tests in certain subjects. Meet with your school counselor for a plan to complete graduation requirements.

If you notice that you are missing the basics or background information needed to understand a new topic/unit in any of your classes, let the teacher know so he can show you what to do to close that learning gap.

The gap may show up as new/unfamiliar material or as a different approach to what is familiar. Sometimes, your performance on a placement test does not indicate this gap. If, on the other hand, you find that a certain subject is too easy for you, let the teacher know as this indicates that you need a more challenging level of the subject. Your transfer will also offer you an opportunity to take more honors and advanced placement courses and it helps your learning to seize such opportunities. At the same time, carry a balanced course load because you are working on academic success and adjusting to a new school environment.

You should, like other students at your high school, monitor your grades, ask your teachers for help as needed, attend free tutoring if your school offers it and you need it. If unanticipated developments arise, contact your school counselor quickly. Get involved in extracurricular activities to build new friendships and ease your adjustment.

If you are homeschooled throughout your high school education, you need to be familiar with the admission requirements of colleges of interest to you and check to see that your homeschooling program meets such requirements. When you start applying to colleges for admission, college admission officers will be looking for supporting documents which include clear evidence that your homeschooling program is accredited by your state and school district and evidence that coursework was completed. Assessment of the coursework should be submitted. Note that colleges tend to prefer the GPA format. You will need your ACT or SAT scores for colleges requiring test scores. The scores need to fit within the range that your colleges of interest normally consider in their selection process.

Be aware that some colleges and universities may handle applications from home-schooled applicants on a case by case basis. Contact the admission offices of colleges that interest you for additional information.

Early Graduation

A very small number of students may decide, for a variety of reasons, to graduate from high school after three years of attendance instead of four. They skip junior year and often take junior year English in the summer. This plan is called waiver of fourth year enrollment, which means graduation after the third year of high school. Students who do this are required to meet graduation requirements like other students and must see their counselor or designated school official to work out the details.

Such students, if they plan on attending four-year colleges, need to find out, before finalizing their early graduation plans, that colleges of interest to them do not discourage early high school graduation. Some colleges do so because of the belief that the student graduating high school early may not be mature enough or ready for college. Such students also bypass taking the PSAT in their junior year, which is when the PSAT counts the most, and because they graduate one year early, they miss out on taking a few more AP and other rigorous courses.

Monitoring Your Progress

Knowing how you are doing throughout your high school career will help you focus and put you in charge of your success. While your parent may request a parent conference a few weeks into any quarter, knowing where you stand in each class will help you and your parent focus on areas where you need to do better. Before your parent arranges a meeting with your teachers, you and your parent need to make sure that:

1. You are doing all class work, homework and applicable labs and projects.
2. You use every opportunity your teacher gives you to get help or to make-up missed work.
3. You get other free tutoring help that your school may offer.

If you are not doing any of these or you tell your parent you've done your assignments when you know you have not, you will hear at the conference that you are failing because you are not doing the work. If you say it's because you don't understand the work, you will have to explain why you did not ask for help. Saying the teacher is "too busy" may reveal the number of times the teacher waited after school to give you help but you simply didn't show up. If your teacher has truly not been able to help you because she has been busy, some arrangement may be made at the meeting to enable you to get the help you need to make progress.

If you monitor your progress correctly, you will always have work done and ready to be given to the teacher. Other students do it. They are not necessarily smarter than you. They are only better organized and want to do well. Depending on how your school handles such issues, you may be able to obtain your grades electronically or directly from your teacher.

A parent conference reveals what you are doing correctly in those classes where you are doing well. It also shows what you need to be doing in those classes where you are not doing well. It would have served its purpose if you use what you and your parent find out to improve your grades.

QUESTIONS FOR STUDENTS

- How do you feel when your parent requests a meeting with your teachers?
- What can you do to decrease the frequency of such meetings?
- If you are in an English Language Learners' (ELL) class, what should you do if you feel that your understanding of English is affecting how well you do in some of your classes?
- If you are from a homeschooling program, what do you want to know about your high school? How will you find out?
- What subjects/courses did you like the most during your homeschooling period? How will you take advantage of similar courses at your high school?

THINGS TO DO

- Consider the things you do that help you in your favorite classes.
- Which of these can you apply to your other classes?
- When will you start?
- If you are in an ELL class, ask your teacher for a list of English books that can help you.
- If you are in some classes with students who speak your original language but have a better knowledge of English, speak with them in English to improve your vocabulary. See your school counselor to discuss your progress and challenges at your new high school.

FOR PARENTS

- How do you decide when to meet with your teen's teacher?
- Which of your teen's teachers would you wish to meet at a parent conference--all or just teachers in classes where your teen is not doing well?
- What is your approach to such a conference--gathering information or blaming one or more teachers for your student's poor performance?
- What will you do to influence your teen if the key reason for her specific poor grades is not doing homework and/or class work?
- What will you do if two or three teachers say that your student finds their classes too difficult because they are honors level classes?
- What will you do if other teachers say your teen finds the on-level classes too easy and needs to be challenged?
- If you are the parent of an international student, ask questions during the enrollment process so that you understand what is expected of your student. Let your student's school know of your plans. For example, will your student be in school for one year only or will he stay in school long enough to graduate?
- If your stay in the United States will be limited, find out what your student needs to graduate and how long it will take. Ask about summer school courses and other options if these will help your student's educational progress and graduation.

CHAPTER 3

ABOUT YOU, YOUR HOME, AND STRESS: COPING WHEN TIMES ARE TOUGH AND REDUCING DISTRACTIONS

My parents divorced when I was in the ninth grade. I'd spend one week with my dad and the next with my mom. My dad lived too far from my school and often drove me to school late. My parents fought again when my mother heard from the school that I was always late and sometimes absent. They both agreed that I stay with my dad only at weekends.
—A high school sophomore

How well do you know yourself? Whatever your answer to that is, you may find, after a brief reflection, that there are things you used to like which you don't like anymore. There may be friends with whom you once had a common interest but the friendship no longer exists because your interests or theirs changed. That's life.

Knowing yourself means that you know

what's important to you and what's not, what to do and what to avoid, how to deal with problems as they arise and how to handle your relationships with others. It means that you need to be ready to end a friendship if it is exploitative or harmful.

You are always changing and you need to know yourself so you can always be yourself. Everyone around you is changing too, your parents, your friends, your teachers and others in your life. Your pictures throughout elementary and middle school confirm this.

The Invisible Backpack

Knowing yourself means being aware of how your surroundings, friends, family and school affect you. It becomes the foundation on which you stand as you make decisions that affect every part of your life.

Because you know yourself, you will know that there are times when you come to school with two backpacks. One is your backpack proper, where you put your school materials. You may carry it all day or leave it in your locker. The other backpack is invisible and sometimes, it feels heavier than the visible one. You and you alone know what's inside it. You keep thinking of it and that's where your mind is when the teacher is teaching. Examples are problems at home, an unresolved conflict with a parent just before you had to leave for school, a sick family member, a grandparent's passing, your missing pet, your family's plan to move next month. What happens when the contents of this invisible backpack fill your thoughts? You can't concentrate at school. How do you get some form of support?

You may begin by telling someone who knows how to listen, for example, your counselor. Depending on how severe the issue is, your counselor may ask to meet with your parent. If this is not helpful because letting your parent know may worsen the problem for you, your counselor may write a report and/or refer your family to a local social services or child welfare agency for help.

When you are having these unpleasant experiences, remember that however understanding your teachers try to be, they must cover the curriculum and so, the work must go on. Your teachers continue teaching and churning out assignments, projects, labs, tests and quizzes whether you are physically and/or mentally there or not. That means you will be responsible for all the work missed in addition to finding a way to get on with the new work.

There are times when carrying this other backpack may mean being sick for a long time. If your parent informs your school, a temporary arrangement can be made to teach you through your school district's home and hospital teaching program.

While this section may not cover every possible scenario you may have to face, the main thing is to know yourself well enough to accept that it is okay to seek support from others and to accept it even if you don't seek it but they offer it anyway.

Another situation arises when you find yourself in a step-family because the parent who has custody has remarried. You may hate your stepmother or stepfather and wonder why you have to welcome a stranger and his/her children into your home or move in with them. You may not necessarily understand your parent's explanation or even care to listen. As far as you know, these strangers will share your parent's affection and it means that you and your original siblings are no longer number one.

This is not an easy situation and may take your entire high school career and beyond to work out. It may involve intervention by extended family members and paid professionals hired by your parent. The resulting stress is likely to affect your school work. Even if you don't feel comfortable discussing this with school staff, you need to understand that your parent may find it necessary and helpful to let your school counselor know about your home situation.

A situation like this may make you hate home and school and not care if your grades fall or not. If your parent does not get help for you, you need to let an adult at your school, most likely your counselor, know. Do this before your situation gets so bad that it leads to self-destructive behavior. Some students in this situation can cope and fit well into the new arrangement. Others may need the help of clinically-trained professionals in community-based social services agencies which help families.

The cause of stress for you may include separating or divorcing parents, separated or divorced parents, single parent, grandparent(s) as parent(s) or something more complex. Sometimes your parents sound like they're trying to stay together because of you. But since they fight all the time and keep you awake and upset most nights, it makes you feel bad and you wish they would just split-up so you can be yourself. When they separate however, you feel guilty though you did not cause their separation. They are dealing with issues which make them no longer compatible and they feel that their best option is to part ways.

When they do, it is painful for you. If you have to live with one parent one week and the other the next and one parent lives twenty miles from your school, your attendance and success in school will be in jeopardy unless your parents reach a joint custody agreement that will not disrupt your education too seriously.

Other Causes of Stress

Courses or course levels that you or your parents choose may result in stress for you. For example, you have always struggled with math but your parents insist that you take an honors level math class. They find you a tutor but you still fail anyway.

If you force yourself into several courses at a more difficult level than you can handle just because your friends are taking these courses, you are heading for stress. Your talents may be in other areas, not in your friends' class choices. If you are taking six difficult courses and you have fall sports practice daily after school and can't find enough time to do all the homework assignments, how will you pass the next set of tests? You've heard too many times a variation of the following, depending on who's talking:

If you don't take several AP and honors courses in high school, no college will admit you. Colleges don't want people who didn't challenge themselves in high school. Colleges don't admit people who took only on-level or college prep classes in high school.

While it is true that taking challenging courses in high school prepares you for college and makes you a competitive applicant, it also makes sense that you take challenging courses in subject areas of your strength. You need to know that you can still go to college, even with a mix of on-level, honors and AP classes.

There are high schools that offer a limited number of AP courses and some honors courses and students from these high schools still gain admission to college. What's more, while your high school transcript is a key factor in college admissions, it is not the only factor on which your admission is based. With over 2,000 colleges and universities in the United States, if you plan well and do your research you will find a college that suits your needs.

You may minimize stress by a wise choice of courses. You may precipitate stress by taking the wrong courses or the wrong levels of the right courses. If you're doing homework or studying for a test until late at night three times a week, your courses may be too difficult or you may have problems with time management. So, how do you manage your time so you can look back at your high school years in the future and remember how exciting they were?

To begin with, you need to rest after you get home from school each day. If you have sports practice, rest after sports practice. Then do a quick scan of your assignment book to see your course assignments. Begin with the ones that are due the next day. From among these, choose the easiest or the least time consuming. Study the notes and class examples. Use your book for further help. Answer the questions.

Tackle the next subject. Avoid spending too much time on one question in any assignment. If a problem presents a challenge, study your notes and class examples to see if they help. If not, contact a student who gets most of the questions right in this class. Ask for hints to help you answer the question and make it clear that you do not wish to write down her solution, that all you want is help so you can answer the question on your own.

If your courses and extracurricular activities are so time-consuming that you can barely get through assignments in two courses each night, you may need to drop some. Sometimes, deciding to do this may be hard. But ask yourself: Are you better off failing two classes and being a top athlete? As you know, this may make you instantly ineligible for sports and you'll have to stop playing for the team until the next report card, provided you make at least a C average then.

As you proceed through high school, you may reflect on some of your experiences since freshman year. You may be tempted to compare yourself to others, a situation which, depending on your temperament, may happen frequently, infrequently, or not at all. You may wish that you look like your best friend, or that your family were like your friend's family. You are you, with all of your strengths and all of your weaknesses. You are unique. You don't have to be an athlete to contribute in a meaningful way to your school community or to succeed in life.

Taking Care of Yourself

How would you like to look when you stand before your mirror so you'll be satisfied with yourself? What can you do to make it happen? Are you ready to undergo the discipline required? Will you do this regularly until you see what you want to be? Will you keep up the practice after getting the results? You may have heard the saying that nature abhors a vacuum. This means you need to replace a bad habit with a good one. It means sticking with the good habit until you do it without thinking about it. No extremes. People have done irreversible harm to themselves because they want to look a certain way. If it is not safe, leave it alone.

If you'd like to change something about yourself, enlist your parents' help. If they feel you need the help of a professional to do it, they may take you to one. But don't experiment with fads or other people's formula. What works for your friend or neighbor may not necessarily work for you. Self-discipline, self-monitoring and a passion for a safe and healthy way of life can do you more good and bring you closer to realizing your personal and academic goals than imitating another person's way of doing things.

Reducing Distractions

You can expect distractions within or outside of school. Distraction may come in the form of disturbing events in your neighborhood. Gang activity, drugs and alcohol may find their way into your life, with unpleasant consequences. A friend or an acquaintance may get into serious trouble which may involve the law. You may want to help but find that there is nothing you can do except to let the friend know that you are there for him or her.

Unless you suffer from some form of

attention deficit that may need the intervention of a professional or are experiencing seriously unstable home conditions, you may find that you and you alone are the only one responsible for creating what distracts you. If you truly want a high school diploma, you shouldn't be sitting down after school, distracting yourself for several hours with activities that do not help you or help others. It's pointless to waste time now and later wish you had not done so. While it makes sense to forget your mistakes of yesterday, repeating them would be a bad choice that will cause you more headaches at home and at school. It's possible to divide your time well between school, sports, other extracurricular activities, play, and friends. This is even easier when you get rid of distractions.

Sports and club membership are not the only time grabbers you may face. They are good because they are not necessarily distractions. Troublesome and distracting are the hours spent in idle chatter on the phone or texting friends, on social network sites, other Internet temptations and on the latest video games. The computer is a fine tool for learning, but it can get in the way of your success if you misuse it. It may even land you in trouble.

QUESTIONS FOR STUDENTS

- What do you do when your life at home is interfering with your education?
- How do you decide when to look for outside help?
- Where do you begin to look?
- Which non-school related activity takes most of your time after school?
- Why do you do it? What can you do to reduce the time spent on this activity?

THINGS TO DO

- On a sheet of paper, write down three things that stress you out.
- On the same sheet of paper, write down what you can do to ease each type of stress listed above.
- Choose two hours one day after school to stay away from television or the use of your computer for recreational purposes. Do other things. How easy or hard did you find it?
- Talk to two or more of your friends with whom you have the same class about starting a study group for that class.

FOR PARENTS

- How will you inform your teen of upcoming changes in your life?
- What will you do to help your teen adjust to these changes?

- How important is it to you that school staff is made aware of your teen's changing home life?
- What does your high school teen spend the most time doing at home?
- Does this stop him from completing/doing school assignments?
- Do you monitor the Internet sites that your teen visits?
- What can you do to help your teen see that doing well in high school depends on giving adequate time to school work?

CHAPTER 4
EXTRACURRICULAR ACTIVITIES

I tried out for the girls' basketball team in my freshman year but got cut. The next year, I made the Varsity Team. That year we were the top team in the county. Practice took so much of my time but I managed to keep up my GPA. It was even better than in freshman year. —A high school sophomore

Whether you're a freshman or upperclassman, whether you're a transfer from another county or another country, you need to find an extracurricular activity that suits your preferences. Some students love sports and they become local, regional, state or even national champions. Some of these students train privately for several hours a week to become highly competitive and may later turn into Olympic or professional stars.

Sports aside, some of the lasting friendships you make in high school may come from your participation in extracurricular activities. Your interest may be in vocal or instrumental music and you may pursue this through the four years of high school. If you started in the elementary grades, you may be at the highest level in music within your first two years or so of high school, or you may be dramatically inclined and start to audition for roles in your school's productions.

If your interest is in community service, develop a volunteer program to assist the elementary school kids or senior citizens in your neighborhood. Volunteer at a local hospital. If you are a musician, you may arrange for a volunteer performance at the same hospital. There are dozens of opportunities for service that benefits others if you're a people person. You may check at your school's career center for volunteer work opportunities. If your school has a volunteer service coordinator, see this staff member. Also, there may be community service clubs at your school which may need volunteers after school.

Focus Your Effort

If you wish to participate in a particular extracurricular activity, be sure it suits your temperament and personality. If it does, put all your energy into it. Enjoy it. Do it well and do it throughout your years of high school.

Be consistent in your participation in extracurricular activities. In other words, go as deep as you can and excel as much as you can in one or two extracurricular activities. This is better than involving yourself superficially in multiple activities without excelling at any of them.

While research has shown that students tend to do well in school when they participate in extracurricular activities, your individual experience will be the best proof of this. Does prominence in extracurricular activities fire you up to do well in class, or are you involved in so many extracurricular activities that you barely have time to study? Are you always struggling to catch up on past work and asking your teachers for extra time to complete projects? If this is so, you need to regroup and examine how you manage your time. You may have taken on far too much than you can handle. If reducing your extracurricular load gives you more study time, then it is smart to do that.

Record your activities, including sports, from the ninth grade. Have a folder or binder to file all information on your extracurricular activities, including details of awards, prizes, and other recognition of achievement. This will prove useful whatever your plans may be after graduating high school.

Note that school is first about your grades and earning that diploma, followed by other matters. No college will recruit any regional or national high school basketball or football or soccer or music star if his grades are so poor that graduation is at risk. Coaches often bear down on their star athletes to perform academically. If the stars get grounded for poor academic performance, the team loses. You know, of course, that as a star performer, you'll be out of the team or other extracurricular activity if you make less than a "C" average each report card time. That's an incentive to do well in school. It's something you owe yourself and nobody else. Of course, you'll make others proud of you because of your accomplishments.

Strengthen Your Team: Build Quality Friendships

In all extracurricular activities, including sports, you are part of a team. This gives you certain opportunities and responsibilities. If your team is weak, you have a duty to work with other members to make it strong. If your team is weak because its individual members are more interested in showing off their individual abilities than in focusing on the team's goal and working together to win, you have an opportunity to refocus the team. You've seen egocentric athletes in professional sports. Their behavior and attitudes are costly to their teams. Each time you say or do something to make team members realize the strength of working together, you demonstrate your leadership, maturity and selflessness. Such action may turn you into team captain. You can do this even if you are in a competitive team outside of school.

Extracurricular activities often widen your circle of friends, as stated earlier. You will notice, therefore, that throughout your high school career, your group of friends change. You find that some of your friends in middle school are drifting away from you, even as you are drifting away from them and making new friends. Because your interests are not what they were last year, you tend to make friends with those who have the same interests as you.

Be open to new friendships that steer you toward better performance in your classes. Keep your distance from friends who skip class and hang out during school hours. You don't know where they are or what they do when they skip class. They may be up to no good. School may be sometimes boring to these kids, but the regret that often follows skipping school is not exciting. They are the ones who get into serious trouble and who may even endanger their own lives. Sooner than later, such students get to know what being in the wrong place at the wrong time means.

Unless you participate in some extracurricular activity which keeps you busy in a social sense, you may be upset when your friends find other friends and abandon you. You know this when they don't return your phone calls or they are always busy when you call. That tells you it's time to find something interesting to do, something that will bring new friends your way. Don't try to play the lone wolf. High school should be fun. But you've got to make it so. Always be open to meeting new people or making new friends.

QUESTIONS FOR STUDENTS

- How many sports and clubs does your school have?
- Which sport or club is your favorite?
- How many hours per week do you spend on it?
- How do you plan your school day so that you can still work on school assignments on days that you participate in sports or other demanding activities?
- How is your extracurricular activity participation affecting your academic progress?
- What can you do to be a greater asset to your team or club?

THINGS TO DO

- If you are not in sports or other extracurricular activity, find out what some of the clubs at your school do, and then see which one matches your interest best.
- Talk to the sponsor. You will enrich your high school experience and meet teens of similar interests by joining a club.

FOR PARENTS

- Which extracurricular activities interest your teen?
- How can you support her in this activity?
- What is the time commitment?
- Can your student manage this activity successfully with school work?

CHAPTER 5
SUCCESSFUL STUDY STRATEGIES

I was pretty much organized and ahead with all my school assignments. But with four AP classes plus an advanced calculus class at our local college, I had to change my study plan. It meant changing to a different part-time job where I worked on Saturdays and Sundays. —A high school junior.

Successful studying requires a plan. If you organize your schoolwork and develop a study plan, you will be successful. This means you should be organized both at home and at school.

Take all material to each class, for example textbooks, pen/pencils, calculator (for math or science), binders plus blank sheets of paper and your planning book. Write down notes on blank sheets and place each set of notes in that section of the binder labeled for that purpose: math for math, history for history and science for science, etc. Write clearly when you take notes. You will be reading your notes later. When taking notes, pay attention to key words and phrases used by your teacher, for example, "remember," "note," "the three most important reasons why," "the two conditions necessary for this to happen are...," "the main characters in this story...," "the causes of this conflict are..."

In history and literature, pay attention to the WHO, WHAT, WHEN, WHY and WHERE of the topic or chapter. The HOW may be important too. For math and science, always keep the HOW in mind. Ask questions when you don't understand. Write down your teacher's answers.

If you'd rather see the teacher privately because you don't want to ask your question in class or because you feel the teacher might say something like, "I just explained that, weren't you paying attention?" write your questions down and arrange to see your teacher later. If you use abbreviations, know what they mean. Copy your teacher's notes exactly.

Be Well-organized

Put homework worksheets in the appropriate section of your binder. In such a case, write, in your planning book, "Math homework: see binder" to remind you to refer to your binder for the math homework worksheet. This may look easy but it's not. Discipline and practice are required to make it work for you. You need to have every homework assignment placed where you can find it and do it. Beyond that, you need to make sure that you bring every completed homework, project and assignment to the appropriate teacher on the due date. If your school runs an after-school and/or lunchtime tutoring program, use it when you need it.

If you have after-school sports practice, use the one hour or more that you have before practice begins to get started on your homework and try to complete as much of it as possible before practice starts. Since playing sports is not a high school graduation requirement, no teacher will excuse your failure to do homework, projects and other assignments because you practice sports for two or four hours after school. If sports or other extracurricular activities are getting in the way of your academic success, you should drop them. If you can't handle academics and sports drop sports. If your GPA falls below 2.0 in any marking period, you are ineligible to participate in most extracurricular activities until your grades improve and put you at 2.0 or better by the next report card. That rule is meant to remind you that your number one reason for attending school is to learn.

Create a Study Schedule

It is important to have a study schedule. Be consistent. Follow it when you get home each day from school. Your schedule may be a variation of the samples below, depending on what time your school day ends and other factors:

2:30-3:30 Snack/Rest
3:30-4:30 Homework
4:30-5:30 Study/Test Prep
5:30-6:00 Rest/Play
6:00-7:00 Dinner
7:00-7:30 Housework
7:30-8:30 Study
8:30-8:45 Place all due assignments in folders. Place folders and books inside your backpack. Get all needed materials, including clothes and shoes ready for next day.

On Sports Practice Days:
2:30-3:00 Rest/Snack
3:00-4:00 Homework
4:00-6:00 Sports Practice
6:30-7:00 Dinner
7:00-7:30 Housework
7:30-8:00 Study
8:00-8:30 Place all due assignments in folders. Put folders and books inside your backpack. Get all needed materials, including clothes and shoes ready for next day.

Some Myths about Homework

You may have heard some or all of the following myths about homework from your peers and others:

"The teacher doesn't grade it. Why bother?"

"The teacher doesn't know whether you got it right or not as long as you say nothing."

"It's not worth the trouble. It's worth only 10 points for the semester."

"Homework? Waste of time. I always get it the first time, why do homework?"

Figured out a way to pass without doing homework? You should write a book on that, or maybe, start your own "Ace the class without doing homework" franchise. Seriously though, you ought to assume that homework tests whether you understand what you are being taught or not. Since you get a homework assignment on every topic of your core classes, you may also assume homework review is a useful test preparation technique though it's not the only one.

The teacher doesn't have to grade your homework. If you don't do it, how will you know if you can do it or not? If you don't do the homework, you won't know which assignments you didn't do correctly. Copying the solution won't help you if you haven't tried to do it in the first place. You may hide your lack of understanding from your teacher but the next test will get you. As for the "It's worth only 10 points" excuse, consider what getting a 70 instead of an 80, an 80 instead of a 90 or a 55 instead of a 65 does to your grade. This kind of homework habit may even render you ineligible for sports or other extracurricular activities.

If you "always get it the first time," pick up a pen or pencil and a blank sheet of paper. Begin now to solve all the problems on your most recent math homework that you didn't do when they were first given, even if the teacher already solved them. Do not look at the solutions. Did you get **ALL** the questions right? Homework is not a waste of time. It's good partial preparation for county and state tests, some of which you may need for graduation. You're not likely to get through any course successfully if you don't do homework. You'll hate your grades. You'll hate yourself. But don't blame the teacher.

If you do your homework and run into difficulty you need to mark the section or point where you got stuck. You could write an e-mail to your teacher or tell your teacher the next day. When that part of the homework you found difficult is explained, you're likely to understand it better. Use your notes, your textbooks and handouts from the teacher when answering homework questions. Smart people do homework.

Preparing for Tests

Each semester, you will take several quizzes and a number of unit tests. The purpose of these tests is to help your teacher find out what you have mastered and where you still need help. Doing well on tests and quizzes will help your overall grade. So, how do you prepare? Before each test, your teacher does a review with the class. Pay attention to what the teacher says on test review day. What's more, write down what your teacher says is "important" or what your teacher writes on the chalkboard about the test.

Know the topic or topics on which the test will be based (content). Listen and take notes as your teacher describes the format of the test, for example, 20 multiple choice questions, 25 true or false questions and five questions needing short answers. Your teacher may give you a breakdown of points totaling 100 or 200 points. Tests are not so intimidating if you prepare by studying everyday and doing all assigned work. Answering additional questions from your textbook or handouts helps even more.

For end-of-semester or final exams, your teachers are likely to give you review packets. You need to know every item in these packets. Ask your teachers if anything is not clear. The goal is to be able to answer all questions based on the content of upcoming tests which may include your review packets, homework, class assignments and examples done by your teachers. As you review, ask questions when you do not understand something. Get tutoring from your teacher or from your school's tutoring program. If you belong to a study group, ask members of your group questions about items you are not sure of and be ready to answer questions from other members.

The SAT and the ACT

For standardized tests like the PSAT, SAT, SAT Subject Tests, the test makers produce free booklets with sample questions to aid your preparation. You may also access websites of the College Board, **CollegeBoard.com,** and ACT Inc, **ACT.org,** to read the information on test format and preparation and try some sample questions. Avoid last minute cramming for any test. This leads to anxiety and poor performance on tests. It makes sense to go to bed early the night before any test. And in the morning, have breakfast.

When you get your test paper and begin the test, read each question carefully.

Understand it before you answer. Do easy questions first. On the PSAT for example, the questions are usually in this order: easy first, followed by more difficult and most difficult. Don't spend twice the time given per question on each question or you'll finish only one-half of the test. Mark difficult questions and go back to them, if you have time at the end of the test and the test rules allow you to go back to earlier questions. Follow all test rules exactly. If you're given bubble sheets, bubble the answer to each question in the proper spot.

QUESTIONS FOR STUDENTS

- How do you handle review packets for tests?
- How do you prepare for a test? Does this work?
- Which study techniques do you use?

THINGS TO DO

- When you receive a graded test, look at it carefully to see why you got the answer to any of the questions wrong. Ask for your teacher's explanation to help you understand those questions that you got wrong.

FOR PARENTS

- What questions do you ask your teen about school tests?
- How does your student prepare for tests, ahead of time or the night before?
- Do you pay compliments to your teen for good performance on a test?
- Do you ask your teen helpful questions about poor test scores?

CHAPTER 6
IT'S ALL ABOUT THE GRADES,
OR IS IT?

Freshman year was easy for me. I got mostly B and A grades. For tenth grade I added honors chemistry, honors pre-calculus and AP Spanish to my other classes. I studied well but everything was just too hard. I was doing assignments until very late at night and I was falling asleep in class. My counselor called a parent conference. My math and science teachers said they felt I would do better if I dropped to regular pre-calculus and chemistry. I didn't want to, but I did. It was fun to understand the classes and start getting good grades again, just like in ninth grade.
—A high school sophomore

As you choose classes, be sure that you can manage your course load. Sometimes you wonder if having A/B grades and a manageable course load "looks" better than two or more grades of C in a rigorous course load. Well, it's a better proof of your diligence and your selection of the right courses that you can earn A and B grades with a rigorous course load than several C grades. A transcript with several honors and a couple of AP classes does not look great with a C average. It certainly looks okay with a B average or better. Go for the AP classes in subject areas where you excel and for the honors level courses where you know that you will find them challenging to a certain extent. Take risks, but do so intelligently. Make the needed effort to do well or excel. For example, if you're not strongly attracted to science, don't go for an AP chemistry course when you barely earned a grade of C in honors chemistry.

Challenge Yourself, Intelligently

Take difficult courses only when you know you can handle them. This means giving more time to studying, of course. If assignments from three advanced courses are forcing you to stay up late just to keep up, you need to consider giving up one of them. If you work after school and you carry a difficult course load, you'll do poorly in your classes if you're too tired to study or to do your homework. If part-time work gets in the way of your grades, drop the part-time work. If you must work, work on weekends only. You are in school to earn a high school diploma, and while part-time work may teach you about interactions in the workplace and put some money in your pocket, it will not get you that diploma and you must let go of work if it stands in your way.

At some point in your high school career, you must consider the message you've been getting from your parents and teachers since your freshman year that "School is about grades." Some of you may accept this. Others are not too sure. Whether you care for it or not, you still have to face it. Your counselor may call you when your grades begin to fall.

You may not even get D or F grades for this to happen. If your grade drops from an A to a C in any class, your teacher may want to know what's going on with you in that class. If it should drop to an F, the feeling is that something is going on with you and it's having a terrible effect on your school work. You may earn failing grades because you are neither studying nor doing any of your assignments. You may be skipping classes or skipping school altogether.

It is also possible to fail by choice if you think it's the only way to get your parent or guardian to pay attention to issues affecting you at home.

Some students fail because they have no clue what's going on in any of their classes. They feel no need to open any of their textbooks. They don't disrupt class. They trouble nobody. They ask no question. They come and go and hope no one notices them. If no one at home is upset by their report cards they hope no one at school is. When their counselors or teachers notice, calls go home to get their parents in and find out why they are not performing.

Failure may also be a result of involvement with illegal drugs and/or alcohol use. This may start as an "experiment." Friends who pressure you to join them may give the impression that everyone is doing it, so it's no big deal. You'll know it's a big deal by the time you find out what this experiment can do to you. You may be hooked and on the way down at top speed. And if you care to look up the statistics, you'll find out that everybody is not doing it.

Ask for Help

You can get academic support in school to help you reverse a downward trend. Getting assistance from teachers and others at school will help you. Understanding what your teachers teach you will help you earn decent grades.

So, how important are grades? Whatever your answer may be, you'll find out when it's time for you to apply to colleges or for post-secondary training that good grades impress the people who are in a position to accept or reject your application or offer you a job or training. There are stipulated minimum GPAs for certain types of postsecondary training and work. When you master thoroughly what is being taught, study and do all assigned work, your grades will reflect your effort and your true ability.

If you earn excellent grades all the time, be proud of your accomplishments. Your dedication to your school work, your successful handling of teenage pressures, and your determination to do well because you believe in yourself and are committed to what you do, will earn you rewards in addition to making you feel good. You are a superior student when you feel good about yourself and your accomplishments. For this, you don't even need to be a straight A student. You just need to be true to yourself and to know that you are doing all you can to be successful.

QUESTIONS FOR STUDENTS

- On a scale of one to ten, ten being most important, how important are grades to you?
- What makes grades that important or not so important to you?
- Why do you do the things that you do? Consider things that you do to please yourself and things that you do to please others.
- Will you do something to please others even if it is harmful to you? Why?
- Which comes easily to you, leading others or following others? Why?
- What do you like about your friends?
- What do you dislike about your friends?
- What would you like to change about your behavior?
- What do you like about the way you deal with issues that affect you?

THINGS TO DO

- On a sheet of paper, write down why you prefer to take your courses at the level(s) you are taking them.

FOR PARENTS

- How do you talk about better grades with your child?
- What can you do to help your teen earn better grades in school?
- What advice do you give your student about friends?

CHAPTER 7
YOUR JUNIOR YEAR

I got an internship after school working at a law firm. In the summer, I would go with the attorneys to court. I really liked it. I took some elective classes at school. I plan to apply to a pre-law program.
—A high school junior

Junior year gives you more opportunities to take challenging courses and work with more focus to raise your grade point average. What you do in your junior year is crucial to your high school career and the college application process.

As you take courses which are more challenging than last year's, you begin to see that sustained effort pays off, even in courses where you're a bit doubtful about doing well. You may think some of your friends are "smart" but you may not be there when they study, ask for help, and then study some more. They shine on tests but they give the impression that they don't study. It looks like they just "know" things. If you choose to investigate, you may find out that they don't spend too much time hanging out at the mall and you may find them doing homework assignments during an indoor track meet. They are usually hard to get when tests and finals are coming up. Once the pace is normal, you see them again.

"Smart" Requires a Plan

If you work part-time, you need to consider how work affects your study/school assignment time. If you work from 4:00 p.m. to midnight three school days a week, your grades will suffer. You may even get your first F grade. If work gets in the way of your high school career, let it go. If you must work, how about working a few hours at weekends?

Being "smart" requires a study plan, asking for help when needed, and sustained effort. It also means taking on what you can handle but challenging yourself to avoid boredom. A good point to start is to believe that it is possible to master a subject by a study plan that fits you and by sustained effort. You cannot know how good you are at something until you try doing it.

When you try, you shouldn't stop just because it is difficult in the beginning. You've got to apply sustained effort. Without sustained effort, success is hard to attain. Having to work hard for good grades does not mean you're not "smart." It does not mean that you don't have talent. Those who think they are smart and have talent will fail if they lack sustained effort.

Ask a professional athlete. When you find out how early these athletes wake up in the morning and for how long they train, you'll know that sustained effort got them to where they are. None of them will ever say that working so hard is proof that they are not "good enough." None of them will ever say that being good enough means training less. If they do that, they will fail. The best among them train year round, allowing themselves to experience, in a week of training, more progress than their less disciplined rivals experience in a month of haphazard training. A defending world heavyweight boxing champion who does not train well enough for the big fight will lose to the unknown underdog who desperately wants to win and who practices with focused sustained effort. Academic and sports champions will gladly tell you how they did it: sustained effort, fueled by an hunger to win.

When your effort is sustained, the results you get are extraordinary. Such results encourage you to move from being an average student to an outstanding student. You smile when the interim report arrives. You're happy when you receive your report card. You are proud of your achievement.

Explore Postsecondary Options

Junior year is the time to visit the career/ college information office at your school. You should begin to gather information on, and explore postsecondary options.

You need to have some idea of the types of colleges that interest you and be able to say whether your evolving academic profile matches what these colleges are looking for in their incoming students. Because college admission involves academic and nonacademic factors, it is reasonable to know which of these colleges to strike off your list as you narrow that list. If, for example, certain colleges have not accepted students from your school with weighted grade point averages of less than 4.0 and SAT scores less than 2000/2400, you know that your weighted GPA of 3.0 plus SAT score of 1600/2400 are unlikely to impress those colleges, unless you are also a national champion in some sports or other activity that interests a department in that college.

Some high school seniors may not plan to attend college immediately after graduation for personal or family reasons. Such students may decide to work or enlist in a branch of the military.

Organizations that employ high school graduates may provide training that can take the most dedicated of these employees to the management level after a number of years.

Students interested in training for an occupation or career with the military need to meet with the military recruiter visiting their high school. The army arranges for these students to take the Armed Services Vocational Aptitude Battery (ASVAB) when they become seniors. The ASVAB test is used to match the applicant's abilities and interests to a Military Occupational Specialty (MOS). Find more information at **www.goarmy.com**. Those interested in the Marine Corps will find more information at **www.marines.com.**

A visit to the counseling/guidance/career information center at your school may provide useful information on other postsecondary options.

Take the PSAT

This is also the time you should take the PSAT to give yourself a shot at qualifying for the National Merit Scholarship Corporation (NMSC) scholarship programs. Taking the PSAT before your junior year is good practice because it allows you to become familiar with the format of the test and with the types of questions asked. If your score puts you in the highest selection index for your state, you may be in line for a National Merit Scholarship.

You need to review your credits at the start of your junior year to stay on track to meet graduation requirements. Again, select your courses with care.

Take Advanced Placement Courses

Try AP courses in your junior year. Choose them in subjects where you do very well. If you're passionate about the sciences, this is a good time to take Advanced Placement courses in chemistry, biology, and/or physics. You may also select AP courses from other subject areas, for example, history and math courses offered by your high school. Remember that AP courses require that you give more of your time to study, writing and research. They are college level courses and the more of them you take, the less academically intimidating your freshman year in college is likely to be. Simply put, AP courses give you better preparation for college.

If your schedule allows it, this is a time to consider taking a science or business internship related to your future plans. Be passionate about the courses you are taking, even if you have not yet decided on a future career or college major. Keep an eye on your time management.

You may enroll in a test preparation class for the SAT or ACT in the fall of your junior year and take one (or both) of these tests in the spring of your junior year. If a SAT prep class is available at your school, take advantage of it if your schedule permits. Let the college entrance tests required by the colleges of your choice guide your decision on whether to take either or both the SAT and the ACT.

Avoid dropping classes because they have now become difficult. It's better not to sign-up in the first place. Before signing-up for a class, ask the teacher about the class and talk to friends who are currently taking it. Your peers are experiencing it from the students' angle and while your experience when you take the class may differ from theirs, what they say is likely to be helpful to you. Continue to monitor your grades closely and do all you can not to fall behind.

The record of your first six semesters of high school plays a crucial role when you apply to colleges in your senior year. Your senior year performance is not being seen at that time. But that does not mean that it's not important. It is, but you need to know that your work through grades nine, ten and eleven make up 75% of your high school career, so they better be great!

QUESTIONS FOR STUDENTS

- In which regular classes did you get mostly A or B grades last school year?
- Did you sign up to take the honors level of these classes in junior year? If not, why not?
- Which of these classes will you take at the AP level? If you did not sign up for an AP level in any of these classes, why not?
- Do you have a study plan in place?

THINGS TO DO

- Find out from your school's counseling or guidance office about gaining access to a free online SAT prep offered by the College Board (if available).
- If your school offers a free after-school or Saturday SAT prep class, sign up.
- Obtain from a bookstore or your local library a book of SAT test practice questions. Use this book to take mock SAT tests at home. Time the tests. Try to simulate ideal testing conditions as much as possible, for example, no phone call or any other interruption.
- Have a parent or guardian score each test for you.

FOR PARENTS

- How can you help your student maintain focus on his academics?

- If time allows, attend your high school junior's parent evening program for information on college admissions.
- Arrange to see your teen's counselor with questions about college and/or career planning for the future.

CHAPTER 8
SENIOR YEAR

I started the fall of my senior year with a GPA of 2.80 which could have been higher if I had not had so many problems through my first three years of high school. My SAT scores were not bad, with a total of 1950. My aunt said I better apply to the community college down the road because no decent four-year college would accept me because of my grades. I did not want to go to a two-year college because I wanted to live in a dormitory and away from home, and because I wanted to stay in the same college for four years if possible, and not transfer. I talked to my counselor. She worked with me and I gained admission to a state university. That's where I'm going next fall. —A high school senior

When you were younger and in ninth grade, you thought twelfth grade was so far into the future that it wasn't worth thinking about. Well, it catches up with you quickly. If you've focused on your studies, prepared yourself for college testing or entered a career preparation program, twelfth grade will not find you wondering what to do with your life after high school.

Last-minute Graduation Plan

If you have simply coasted along and never really cared to understand why anyone should be interested in doing well in high school, you may be so much behind that graduating on time, even with the lowest GPA possible, becomes an extremely difficult task.

Senior year is payback time for all those poor choices. It may also be the time to formulate a graduation plan for those who cannot meet graduation requirements by June. Summer school classes, evening classes in the fall, perhaps another semester or year at your school become important options.

If you check your local newspapers or talk to employers, you'll find that your job prospects won't look good without a high school diploma. This may explain why some of those General Education Diploma (GED) classes fill up quickly. To be eligible for most, if not all postsecondary training programs, you've got to have a high school diploma or its equivalent.

Settling for a minimum wage job won't get you very far because you'll put yourself in a situation where you always need more money than you can earn. If you think school is "a waste of time," try asking those who dropped out and now work at minimum wage jobs.

Don't Slack-off!

Your senior year transcript is the final academic record that provides evidence that you have completed your high school education. While the record of your first six semesters of high school is what the admissions personnel of colleges see when you apply, your twelfth grade course load is an indicator of your desire to continue taking very demanding courses and your continuing preparation for the challenging academic program that awaits you in college.

It is very important, therefore, that you select your senior year courses with care. Contrary to whatever you may hear from some of your peers, senior year is **NOT** the time to slow down or take fluffy courses. If you are preparing for college or postsecondary training, you need to take demanding courses to be competitive. Beyond that, mostly easy level core and elective courses will render you unprepared for college or advanced training. It may lead to frustration and cause you to drop out of college later.

Some high school seniors often say that all they need in senior year is the last credit of English required for graduation. It is assumed that they are also sensible enough to realize that even if their state or district allows them to take only English in their senior year, they should do better than that to be prepared for college or for life. A next to zero senior year course load, like English 12/English IV plus an elective class may even jeopardize your chances of getting a decent job after graduation.

The need to take courses that matter in your senior year must be stressed until you feel like screaming when one more person tells you, "Don't slack off now. It's stupid." Of course, scheduling constraints and conflicts at your school may make it impossible for you to get one or two great courses you'd really love to take in senior year. You may have to sacrifice one of them to take the other. If time permits and transportation is not an issue, you may take the conflicting course at another high school or even under a dual enrollment or early placement program at your local community college.

Consider this senior year assumption: "I

got an A third quarter. If I do nothing and fail fourth quarter and the final exam, I'll still pass the class." Whether you need that class for graduation or not, you'll be in for an unpleasant surprise when you learn that your final grade in that class is an F. If you think it doesn't matter, be prepared to answer some embarrassing questions from those who will look at your transcript.

Here is another assumption: "I don't need the class. It's an elective. It doesn't matter if I fail it." Well, fail it you did. Then that F appeared on your final transcript and put a question mark on your college aspirations. Which college wants a student who cannot be counted upon to complete his course load successfully? Barring unforeseen personal circumstances that might have affected your high school grades, every low/failing grade you earn, especially in your senior year indicates that you cannot be depended upon to finish what you started.

If you feel you must have a light load to survive your senior year, consider attending school for a half-day and having an internship for the second half of the day. You may also check to see if your school permits seniors to attend classes for a half-day and work for the rest of the day. This may motivate you to do well in the few classes you are taking.

General Graduation Requirements

Because state universities and colleges tend to base their minimum requirements for admission on the state's high school graduation requirements, which may be lower than each county or school district's graduation requirements, you may count on some variation of the following as requirements for a high school diploma in most school districts:

- English (4 years/4 credits)
- Math (3 or 4 years/3 or 4 credits, may include algebra, geometry and Algebra 2/ Advanced Algebra)
- Science (3 years/3 credits, may include biology and a physical science)
- History/Social studies (2 or 3 years/2 or 3 credits)
- Physical education (.5 or 1 year/.5 or 1 credit)
- Health (.5 or 1 year/.5 or 1 credit)
- Computer literacy/technology (1 year/1 credit)

- Foreign language (1 or 2 year(s)/1 or 2 credit(s) **or**
- Career Tech/Vocational Tech prep or 1 or 2 credits of advanced tech
- Art/Music/Drama (1 year/unit)

Attaining a passing score on a state-mandated competency/exit exam in selected core subject areas may be required. A stipulated number of hours of community service is a graduation requirement in most school districts.

Some high school seniors slow down after the first semester of senior year, letting their grades drop and exhibiting behavior that teachers who know them well find strange. If this happens due to circumstances beyond their control, they need to make appropriate school staff aware of this and/or get help through other agencies.

However, it must be emphasized again that high school seniors who stop doing their school work under the pretext that it's their senior year or that they've never really had any fun in high school need to know that the fun disappears when they are listed as non-graduates. They risk having college offers of admission withdrawn and losing scholarships due to their poor grades. They are proving how unreliable they are and weakening their college readiness. Parents and other family members need to remind such seniors to keep working until their final exams are done.

Beyond grades, school is a mini-society which tests your ability to handle conflicts with your fellow students or your social circle. Challenges in relationships will come your way, even with best friends, teammates and others in your extracurricular activities and academic classes. Facing and overcoming the many obstacles that come your way in high school will help you build strength and make you unique as an individual. It may even give you a reputation as the one who is always there for others, who is an expert at resolving conflicts, and who keeps the group united.

QUESTIONS FOR STUDENTS

- What do you risk by failing classes after spring break?
- Looking back at the last four years, what did you like the most about high school? Why?

THINGS TO DO

- If you feel less motivated and are tempted to skip class, miss assignments and attract negative attention from your teachers, consult your counselor.
- If you are at risk of failing a class required for graduation, see the teacher.
- From your freshman year to the present, list three things you think you did best. List three things you could have done better. State how this can help you after high school.

FOR PARENTS

- How do you ensure that your high school senior maintains decent attendance and grades through her senior year?

PART TWO
A COLLEGE ADMISSIONS PRIMER

CHAPTER 9
GETTING READY FOR COLLEGE:
A TIMELINE

Ninth Grade

Sign-up for academic courses at a level that you can handle: English, algebra or geometry, science, social studies, foreign language. Get to know your counselor. Select an extracurricular activity that you're passionate about and start a log of all your extracurricular activities and summer programs. You may take the PSAT for practice if your school allows ninth graders to take it. Develop superior study and organization skills. Keep an eye on your grades. Study daily. Get help when you need it. Do all assignments. Read several books all year, especially in the summer, to build your vocabulary. If your high school gives summer assignments in any subject, look out for them and do them all.

Tenth Grade

While selecting courses that you can handle, include a few challenging ones. Study daily. Do all assignments. Monitor your grades. Always ask for help from your teachers and get tutoring assistance when needed. Continue with your preferred extracurricular activities and record them. Get to know your counselor. Get involved in a summer activity that benefits others. Get a summer job just for the experience. Find out more about colleges that interest you by visiting your school's college and career information center. Take the PSAT for practice. Research a few colleges of interest. Read, read, read and keep your grades on an upward trend.

Eleventh Grade

By now you would have heard that "Junior year is the hardest of all." Juniors say so because that's the time when all of their school's most rigorous courses, including Advanced Placement courses, are open to them. Not surprisingly, that's also the time when juniors begin to overload themselves with these rigorous courses. Select rigorous courses, including AP courses if your school offers them, in subjects you enjoy, not just because such courses will "look good for college." Monitor your grades. Continue with your extracurricular activities. Take the PSAT in the fall. If your Selective Index is high for your state, it may place you in the running for a National Merit Scholarship. Visit colleges you think you might want to apply to as early as spring. It makes sense to know what you are looking for on a college campus when you visit. Note your impressions. Prepare for the SAT. If your school offers a SAT prep class which fits with your schedule, take it. Continue with your extracurricular activities in and/or outside of school.

Twelfth Grade

Give time and thought to preparing your college applications so that they represent you in the best possible way.

Your senior year courses must continue to show that you are preparing for college. The more demanding they are the better. Include AP courses if your school offers them. While your academic record during the first six semesters of high school is crucial to your college application process, your course load in the twelfth grade counts too. If you apply regular decision like the majority of applicants, certain colleges you apply to may require mid-year grades. This allows them to see that you have not dropped some of the rigorous classes on your schedule at the time you submitted your application. It also shows your first semester grades. When colleges admit you either through Early Action, Early Decision or regular decision, they usually ask that you maintain the same level of academic performance that earned you that acceptance.

Slacking off, dropping courses that have now become difficult because you are studying less and less, missing school for no reason, skipping some classes to hang out with friends who lack discipline may not only put your college acceptance at risk, such behavior may jeopardize your graduation. Being a senior sluggard may be costly to you.

Visit the top two or three colleges which offered you admission before you pay your deposit on May 1. Arrange with the admissions office to spend a couple of nights. If alumni from your high school are there and you know them, ask if they don't mind hosting you for a couple of days.

CHAPTER 10
COLLEGE ADMISSION:
WHAT YOU NEED TO KNOW

After you've done your research and before you start applying to colleges, you need to be aware of some facts if you are aiming for admission by a selective school. The term "selective" as used here is relative. Some of your state's universities may be selective. A college that is selective for you may not be as selective for your friend whose academic and total profile differ a great deal from yours.

If you and your friend are in the same high school, apply to the same college and your friend's transcript lists seven Advanced Placement courses while yours lists only two, a selective college admissions officer reviewing your transcripts and your school profile sees immediately that your friend has made more use of academic opportunities offered by your school. Your friend gains an instant advantage. You may think you've compensated for your fewer demanding courses by extracurricular activities and leadership in student government, but while selective colleges maintain that they seek a diverse student body with a wide range of talents and experiences, their feeling that excellence in rigorous coursework is an indication of potential college success won't dissolve easily. Your friend may be admitted while you are denied admission. This does not mean that you won't gain admission to a good four-year college. It only means that you need to be ready for some disappointments. The more selective the college is, the higher your risk of being denied admission.

Highly Selective Colleges

Top colleges have room for only a fraction of the well-qualified students who apply for admission each year. Perfect SAT/ACT scores and a perfect GPA on a transcript which shows the most rigorous courses available may not and do not guarantee admission. Add two hundred such students to the applicant pool at the same selective college, with similar extracurricular activities (music, drama, debate, student government, and others) plus awards and honors, and you have a situation which makes selection difficult for admissions staff of this college but does not make your acceptance as a top notch, well-rounded student any easier. It may sometimes seem like the admission of top achieving students to such colleges is based on the toss of a coin.

Your school being one of the top ranked in the nation is also not a guarantee of admission at these highly selective colleges. A high school that's top ranked may have as many as 25 students in its number one slot. Think of all the number one students in so many high schools applying to these same colleges for admission.

The number of admits from the applicant pool decreases as the numerical rank or percentile rank of high school seniors increases. In other words, highly selective colleges will accept a higher number of students in the top five percent of their high school senior class and a lower number of students who rank between the top six percent and the top ten percent. Check current profiles of entering freshman classes at some of these colleges from their websites.

Because you are in competition with other academic standouts who also have solid track records in extracurricular activities, you need to have achieved something truly outstanding or unique to distinguish you from the crowd. This may sound frustrating and you are probably asking, "Is all this necessary for me to gain admission to my favorite college?" The answer is a qualified "yes." Let your passions, let what you care about and how you've cared about it, speak for you. This is why you need to focus on extracurricular activities that interest you immensely, rather than get involved in activities which you think "will look good for college."

You are likely to make a significant contribution and perhaps, improve the lives of others if you are in activities you care about. You will stand out. Consider your high school courses too. What is unique about a course or courses you have taken? Are you one of only fifteen students in an advanced mathematics or science class at your school? Have you taken a strong position on an issue or are you committed to one? What makes you unique? What do you do in a unique way?

A Commonsense Approach

Treat college admission the same way you treat daily life. In life you don't have your way all the time and saying "it's not fair" isn't going to change that. If you've gotten your way so far be grateful, but be prepared for that day or that time when you will not get your way.

When you apply to several colleges, be realistic and know that you risk being denied admission by some of them. You may already know that you don't have the "stats" to get into certain colleges but you apply anyway, just in case.

Believe it or not, a college may deny you admission because its admission committee is convinced that you will not accept its offer of admission because you are over-qualified. The committee reasons that it's better to "give that spot to someone who really needs it and will attend."

"But how can they know that?" you groan.

They don't in your case. They are relying on years of experience with overqualified applicants whom they've admitted but who did not attend. There are times when they will be wrong, times when they will reject the overqualified student who truly wants to enroll if admitted. On the flip side, prepare yourself for the triumphs of admission. If you have done your research and worked closely with your high school college adviser, it will happen. But prepare also for the discouragement that comes from being denied admission. For that will happen too.

You may find yourself in that rare situation where every college to which you apply offers you admission even if you thought the first two were certainly "reach" schools for you. This may surprise you. But know that the key elements of your entire application played a major role here. So did the needs of those top two "reach" colleges to have a balanced freshman class. "Balanced" changes in meaning for these colleges from one admission season to the next. That's the part you won't be able to figure out, try as you may. Perhaps considering that each year, selective colleges reject dozens of applicants whose profiles match those of the applicants they accept may help you understand this a bit.

Diversify Your Search

Do not pin your hopes of attending a four-year college on one and only one college. If that one college denies you admission, what will you do? Identify, research, visit and apply to colleges which fit your personal criteria and academic profile. You may include a couple of colleges which are in the "reach" range for you, about three which seem to be within range and another three which look like they will admit you. Do not label any college as your "safety school."

It is your task to know the admission requirements of each college of interest to you before you apply. Study its website. Review its viewbook. Communicate with its admission personnel. Does it recalculate GPA? If so how? How does it use SAT/ACT scores if it requires them? Which or how many SAT Subject Tests does it require? Does it help your application to visit its campus before applying?

Find out what level and how many years (units) of core courses it expects its applicants to have completed before enrolling in college. For example, some colleges require that you complete trigonometry while others may require three years of a foreign language. Some ask for two lab sciences. There may be a degree of flexibility in some requirements, depending on the rest of your transcript. Find out. That's your duty!

What Does It Take to Get In?

An assistant admissions director of a medium-sized state university in Maryland informed me that the first thing her admissions committee looks at is the applicant's transcript, followed by test scores (SAT, ACT). If the student is close to being accepted, the committee asks for senior year grades or additional test scores. If the university is still not sure about making a decision, they consider the applicant's entire profile, rigor of classes, essay, recommendations and activities. For GPA, they recalculate and use their own formula to weigh grades for AP, IB, and honors classes. The transcript is the most important factor, followed by the difficulty of courses taken and the test scores, both of which have the same degree of importance. Next come the essay and letters of recommendation, which have the same degree of importance, followed by an evaluation of how well the application was completed. Extracurricular activities come next.

Admissions officials from several colleges in the South stress the importance of the transcript, rigorous courses and good scores on the SAT/ACT and being in the top 20% or 25% of the senior class. They expect students to start taking challenging courses from ninth grade. Some of these officials say that it helps to apply Early Action while others say that it may be harder for some applicants to get in through Early Action if the Early Action applicant pool is highly competitive.

The above indicates that college bound students need to take rigorous courses and do well in them, have good test scores, fill out their applications thoughtfully, write essays which only they can write, and have a passion. They need to be mindful of deadlines and have a well-organized filing system to track their applications. For this, a filing system in categories similar to the ones below might help:

Colleges
Date Applied
Date Transcripts Sent
Visited--impression

CHAPTER 11
COLLEGE ADMISSION: WHICH COLLEGE IS RIGHT FOR YOU?

Before you begin your college search, it makes sense that you should know what you are looking for. When you were in eighth grade in middle school, you knew you would go to the high school for which your middle school served as a feeder school. If your family were moving, you knew you would go to a new and, maybe, very different high school. In this case, you could not have stayed behind to attend your area high school just because your best friend was going to attend that school.

While circumstances may be different when you start applying to colleges, your college choice will depend on a number of factors, but not on attending the same college as your best friend. If it happens by coincidence, fine. But the college admission landscape is so complex and dependent on so many variables that attending the same college as your best friend or your twin brother or sister may or may not be crucial to the process for you.

College Search: Guide Questions

You need to begin your search by determining which college is the right one for you. You need to know yourself to do this well. For a start, answers to the questions below will help you identify what you are looking for in a college.

- In what part of the country would you like to study?
- What size of college population interests you? (Examples: small liberal arts, medium-size, or large public university).
- Are you interested in an urban or rural location?
- Is the reputation of a college in a particular major of interest to you? (Example: engineering, film, journalism, theater. Be mindful that competition can be stiff for those majors in these colleges.)
- Is religious affiliation a factor in your

college search?
- Co-educational, men only, or women only?
- Are school spirit and sports important to you?
- Is cost a major factor for you?
- What is your GPA, weighted and not weighted?
- What are your SAT scores on the Critical Reading, Math and Writing tests?
- What are your scores on the ACT?
- How do your SAT and/or ACT scores compare with those of seniors from your school who were admitted to colleges of interest to you in the past three years?
- Are you interested in colleges that provide additional support for students with learning disabilities?
- How have you done college research so far: websites? Which ones? Books? Which ones?

Study College Profile Pages

After you've answered these questions to help you identify what sort of college environment will be right for you, the next thing is to see what chances you have of being admitted by the colleges you are considering.

The profile pages of a college's website may help you find an answer. It will list, among other facts, how many applications the college received (Early Decision, if applicable and regular decision). How many applicants were admitted (Early Decision, regular decision) and of these, how many were top 5%, top 10% and top 20% of their senior classes. It may also show a below 20% and a test score range (SAT, ACT) for the middle 50% of its admitted applicants. Note these numbers and see where you fit. But you are not done yet. From your school's college admission database, obtainable from your counselor, ask to see what the GPA and SAT scores of your high school's applicants to that college over the past three or four years look like. You will now have sufficient information to help you decide if it's worth your while applying to that college.

Now that you've settled on a list of colleges to apply to, which should include about three which your profile fits easily, three which you think may be hard for you to get into, and three which you feel may be extremely difficult for you to get into (reach), but to which you still want to apply anyway, just in case, you are ready for the next stage. But before that, how "reach" are your reach schools? If these are colleges which accepted three students with 4.0 GPA (not weighted) and SAT scores between 2250 and 2400 from your school and rejected twelve others with slightly lower academic statistics in the past three years, it is reasonable to ask you to hold on to your application fee if your GPA is 2.99(not weighted) and your SAT score is 1850. Unless you have an extraordinary talent in a special area or you are a national sports champion whom these schools are interested in, you are unlikely to be admitted.

Begin your research on the schools which are of interest to you. Get all the information you can from their websites. Get their catalogs. If possible, interview alumni of your high school who are now undergraduates at these schools. Plan visits to these schools.

The College Visit

The spring of your junior year, the summer before and the fall of senior year are good times to visit colleges. The college visit brings you face to face with the physical environment of the college and its ambience. If it's in the spring or fall, you'll find students whom you can ask questions. Ask them what they like best about the college. Ask what irks them about it. While you may not share similar tastes with the undergraduates who are answering your questions, you'll begin to get a sense of whether you'd like to spend the next four years at this school or not. You'll see and feel what the catalog, viewbook and website cannot convey to you.

If the environment outside the campus matters to you, your visit shows you what it's like. How safe do students feel on campus? What is campus life like at weekends? What are the students like? You may not have an answer to this particular question unless you stay for two days or so by arrangement with the admissions office. You may find students are from different parts of the country, open-minded and friendly. If students tend to be in groups or cliques and seem to be products of the same type of private high schools, you may feel excluded and that may lead you to drop that school from your list. You'll need to note all your observations for each college visit so that when those acceptance letters arrive, you'll be able to decide wisely.

Community Colleges

Community colleges offer programs that prepare students to transfer to four-year colleges after completing a program of study successfully. They also prepare students for careers which include healthcare, technology and information science.

Community colleges should not be thought of as the colleges established for those who performed poorly in high school, though for some students the two-year college may be the only sure route to higher education. The mission of the community college is broader.

Some community colleges offer two-year concentrated programs in the sciences and technology. Admission to such programs is very competitive and may come with special scholarships for selected applicants. Some top academic achievers in high school opt for such programs to stay closer to home, save money and get a superb college education for two years. They transfer to a four-year college and may earn another scholarship to complete their undergraduate studies.

Community colleges also give students who scraped through high school the opportunity to polish their study habits. Counselors at these colleges help these students plan academically to bridge the gaps in their learning. Counselors use placement tests to help them select appropriate courses. These students may study for careers or prepare to transfer to a four-year college upon the successful completion of an associate degree.

Community colleges are also of great benefit to high school graduates with limited English proficiency. Such students get support to improve their English and may earn an associate degree and transfer to a four-year college later.

CHAPTER 12
THE COLLEGE APPLICATION

Before you fill out a college application form, you have to decide which of the available application options is best for you. These options are Early Action, Early Decision, regular decision and rolling admission.

For Early Action, you apply by the deadline, for example December 1, and you get a decision within an announced period of time. You have until May 1 to decide, if admitted, whether to attend or not. Early Action is non-binding and leaves you free to apply to other colleges. Find out from each Early Action college of interest what restrictions, if any, are imposed on Early Action applicants. Some Early Action colleges may require that an admitted student withdraw applications from other schools, making this option sound like Early Decision.

When you apply Early Decision, you still apply by the publicized deadline. You must enroll if admitted. Your application deadline and decision date may be, for example, October 15 and December 15 respectively. Early Decision is binding.

Regarding regular decision, you apply by the deadline and you get a decision within a publicized period of time. It is non-binding.

With rolling admission, colleges review applications as they are submitted and notify applicants during the admission period. It makes sense to apply to a school with rolling admission as early as possible. Rolling admission is non-binding.

Know your deadlines for each of the plans and stick with the instructions given by each institution. If you are not clear as to what an institution means by the implications of applying under a certain plan, contact its admissions office to ask for clarification.

For Early Decision and Early Action, if you are sure that you won't have new academic or other achievement information to present after the deadline, and you are absolutely certain, after visiting that college and interviewing some of its undergraduates that this is the one school that you care the most about attending, send in your application.

Will an Early Decision application necessarily improve your chances of admission?

Maybe, depending on the school, the profile and number of Early Decision applicants during a particular admission season and the number of slots the school has to fill for its incoming freshman class. Look up the profile of colleges of interest to you and see what the numbers are for Early Decision applicants and admits as well as regular decision applicants and admits. If you're looking at the percentages, note that the number of regular decision applicants is always higher than that of Early Decision applicants.

Admissions officers at selective schools often insist that the students they admit Early Decision would have been admitted regular decision. Sometimes this seems so. At other times, it's hard to be so sure. Either way, if you've decided that a particular school truly stands out as the place where you'd like to study for the next four years, and you're sure that your credentials are as solid now as they will be six to eight weeks from now, why not apply Early Decision?

If, however you'll need an October SAT on which you hope your scores might be better, and you're waiting to clinch a national championship in some activity in the fall, you should apply regular decision.

How Many Colleges?

How many schools should you apply to? If you do a thorough research, eight to ten schools are fine. Include two or three that you know may be "reach" schools, about four that may be within your range but which you'll attend if admitted and two or three for which your academic profile is above their averages. Avoid thinking of any particular school as a "safety" school. If your "safety" school receives an unprecedented surge in applications because of a newly acquired status in sports or a new ranking that gives it a spot among top schools, it may turn down hundreds, maybe thousands of applicants who think it's their "safety" school. Some students apply to twenty or more schools. After the results come in, how many schools can one student attend?

Completing the Application

Every college application asks you for personal, family, educational, test type and test score information. You will also have to list your extracurricular activities both within and outside of school, your citizenship status and place of birth.

You will give information about your parent(s)' education and occupation and whether you live with one or both parents. You will list jobs you've done and internships you've served or are serving. Answer all questions. If a question does not apply, write "not applicable" but otherwise leave no question unanswered. Be honest. If you've been expelled from a school, say so and explain the circumstances.

If you are applying Early Decision, you need to sign the Early Decision section of the application as directed and give your parent/ guardian to sign. It will require your counselor's signature too. Sign and date your application as instructed. You may include a single page of activities and key roles, especially leadership roles you played. Make sure that your application is free from error.

The Essay

Here's that section of your college application about which you can do something right now. You cannot change what's on your transcript and while you can hope that you score 100 points more overall in your fall SAT, it is possible that your score increases by twenty points or decreases by twenty points when compared to your June score. But you can write an essay which allows admissions personnel to get to know you, the individual behind the application. Although that one item by itself does not necessarily determine whether you get in or not, it can help sway a decision in your favor.

The essay allows you to focus on yourself and reveal as much or as little as you want about yourself. It needs to be treated like the one thing that must now be done well since it is within your control. While your English teacher takes you through the mechanics of the college essay, its style, content and writing are up to you.

The Interview

If some of the colleges of interest to you include an interview as part of the application process, you need to be prepared for the interview. Interviews may be alumni or admissions office interviews. They may be formal or informal. They may be structured and used as another tool to decide who is admissible and who is not. It's important to be well prepared for the interview, even if you don't know how it will be used or how much it will help your application.

Whether your interview is on campus, at a private residence or at a local café, get there on time. Be ready to answer questions about why you are applying to that particular college, about your passion, and about your favorite subject at school. If it's an on-campus interview, some of the questions you get may be based on what you wrote on your application. If it's your number one school, let your enthusiasm show in your answers. If it's a back-up in case your number one school doesn't work out, be careful how you answer when asked if it's your top choice school. If you say that it is one of the schools you're considering seriously that will suffice.

As relevant questions come up, highlight your achievements without sounding arrogant. Reveal aspects of your nature that make your teachers admire and respect you. Remember to thank your interviewer after the interview. If you've decided on a question to ask, ask it. Ask only questions whose answers are not on the college's website or catalog. Demonstrate, as much as you can, an adult level engagement.

It's normal to be nervous at a college admission interview. This is why you need to prepare for it. It helps if you can find someone with whom to rehearse. While interviews are not limited to the sample questions below, practicing with them by having an adult, preferably your school counselor if possible, ask you these questions may help to put you in the proper frame of mind for the interview.

- Tell me about yourself.
- What will the teachers who know you well say about you?
- Are we your first choice?
- How did you decide that our college/university is a good fit for you?
- Where else are you applying?
- What do you like best about your high school?
- What do you like the least about your high school?
- What do you think needs to be done to correct it?
- Which of your high school activities do

you wish to continue in college? How will
you do this?
- Which of your high school courses do you
find most interesting? Why?
- What do you see yourself doing ten years
from now?
- What are you looking to gain from attending our college/university?
- What words of wisdom would you have
for a freshman at your school?

Selective college interviews for prestigious
scholarships awarded by certain colleges are
far more rigorous than general admission interviews and may include two or more elimi-
nation rounds before the final stage.

Such interviews, like admission interviews, may begin with what you have written on your application. Members of the
interview panel get you to relax before firing
the tough questions at you. Their questions
test how you think and reason. A committee
member of a prestigious scholarship program at an Ivy League university gave me examples of such questions: "What is the most
difficult issue your generation faces and how
will you solve it?" "If you were to write your
autobiography fifty years from now, what

would its title be?" If you think you did very well on these two examples, consider this one: "What is the value of funding for the arts in public schools when several students in these schools lack core math, reading and writing skills?" How will you defend your position as you answer this question?

A structured admission or scholarship interview is designed to identify your passion. While having something you are truly passionate about is fine, it is even more important that you convey that passion in a highly infectious manner. Your passion does not necessarily have to be something grand. It may be something that thrills you in such a way that when you speak about it, you radiate an energy that compels your audience to take an interest in what you are saying. This is something you should be able to speak about clearly and enthusiastically. It must also be something that makes you proud. If you are shy, you will need to practice, perhaps with a parent and/or your counselor as your audience until you succeed in getting your audience absorbed in what you are saying. If speaking about your passion makes your interviewer or members of the interviewing panel yawn, know that there is a problem.

Be ready to talk about other things you've done. If you wrote about your favorite author or favorite book on your application or essay, be ready to discuss either briefly. Some questions they throw at you may require that you pause. Don't be in a hurry to give an answer. It is okay to say "Please give me a few moments." If your pause is prolonged, your interviewer will prompt you with a comment.

Recommendations

Some of your applications may require two recommendations from your teachers. Select and ask academic subject teachers who know you very well to write these for you. These may not necessarily be subjects in which you had "A" grades though there is no harm in these being so. Choose teachers who know you for your contribution in class, your creativity and who see you leading in group-work and explaining steps or processes to your peers. You can also request an additional recommendation from your extracurricular activities advisor. This person may know you for your leadership skills, energy and ease in getting the group or the team to move as desired. In that same category is a recommendation from a professional with whom you served an internship in the summer or for a whole year. These will be enough.

Your counselor's recommendation is so important that it makes sense to get to know your counselor well before your senior year. Secondary School Report forms from most colleges ask your counselor to check how often he sees you and/or how well he knows you. A recommendation from the counselor who knows you will include anecdotal and specific information that may reveal your strengths to the admissions officer in a way that no other individual could. Admissions officers may call your counselor even if you are a top student as long as there is a need for them to do so. Your school counselor becomes your strongest advocate if you've allowed him to get to know you very well.

Once you've done your part with each of your application, making sure that you observed all deadlines, that you requested transcripts following your high school's instructions for doing so, that you sent portfolios and other supporting documents as directed and that you recorded in a separate folder, the order and dates on which you did these things, you may relax.

CHAPTER 13
FUNDING YOUR
COLLEGE EDUCATION

The concern that your family cannot afford to pay the full cost of your college education should not prevent you from applying to college.

If your GPA and SAT scores are outstanding, check to see if your colleges of interest have merit scholarships. These may have different names but the criteria often include academic excellence and other requirements. If you are eligible, ask your counselor to nominate you if such scholarships require this. Apply by the deadline.

As you complete each application, check the website of the college to see what information it has on financial aid and scholarships and what its deadline is for financial aid applications. You will need to complete the application for financial aid and return it to each college by the deadline once you are admitted. After you receive financial aid award information from the colleges that admitted you, you and your parents may compare these financial aid packages before you decide where to go, which may not be the college asking you to pay the least amount of money.

Free Application for Federal Student Aid (FAFSA)

To be considered for any form of financial aid for postsecondary education, you must complete and file a Free Application for Federal Student Aid (FAFSA) as soon as possible after January 1 of your senior year. Doing this after your parents have filed their federal income tax returns, provided they file early, may save time because information entered from your parents' tax returns will be exact, not estimates. Otherwise, estimates may be used and later corrected when the returns are filed. The point is to file the FAFSA early.

The U.S. Department of Education provides financial aid for eligible students embarking on postsecondary education. Some of these requirements call for the student to be a citizen of the United States or an eligible non-citizen, to have a high school diploma and to enroll as a regular student in an eligible degree or certificate program. Most male students must register with Selective Service to receive federal student aid and may use the FAFSA to do so. Students may register online at **www.sss.gov**. For a comprehensive list of eligibility requirements, it is strongly recommended that students and parents/ guardians consult the Student Eligibility volume of the Federal Student Aid Handbook in the "Publications" section of **www.ifap. ed.gov.**

For eligible students, financial aid includes the following:

Grants: (Federal Pell Grants, Academic Competitiveness Grants, National Science and Mathematics Access to Retain Talent [SMART] Grants, Federal Supplemental Educational Opportunity Grants (FSEOG). Grants do not have to be repaid except in special circumstances.

Loans: (Perkins, Direct and Federal Family Education Loan [FFEL]. The Federal Perkins Loan is campus-based. Direct loans are:

- Federal Direct Stafford Loans (for students, subsidized).
- Federal Direct Stafford Loans (for

students, unsubsidized).
- Federal Direct Plus Loans (for parents and graduate or professional students).
- Federal Direct Consolidation Loans (to combine federal education loan debts).

The following are Federal Family Education Loans:

- Federal Stafford Loans (for students, subsidized).
- Federal Stafford Loans (for students, unsubsidized).
- Federal PLUS Loans (for parents and graduates or professional students).
- Federal Consolidation Loans(to combine federal education loan debts).

For more information, visit **www. FederalStudentAid.ed.gov** and you may also obtain and read *Funding Education Beyond High School: The Guide to Federal Student Aid* obtainable from **www. FederalStudentAid.ed.gov/guide** and for links to other government programs, visit **www.students.gov.**

State Aid

Since each state administers its own student aid programs, you should contact your state education or higher education agency for information on available student aid for postsecondary education.

Individual Colleges and Private Organizations

Individual colleges and universities offer aid for which the Free Application for Federal Student Aid (FAFSA) must be submitted in addition to the school's own application for financial aid. You may obtain more information on this from the college's financial aid office.

Students who may be eligible for private grants or scholarships for academic achievement, community activities, athletic ability or ethnic/racial heritage can access the Federal Student Aid website at **www. FederalStudentAid.ed.gov** for a free scholarship search.

About 70 percent of all financial aid awards come from federal and state programs listed in *Funding Education Beyond High School: The Guide to Federal Student Aid* and other free publications.

The U.S. Department of Education tells parents/guardians and students to be wary of the value of the search being offered by commercially operated financial aid services which tend to be very expensive.

Financial Need

The student's financial need, once he/she meets eligibility requirements is the difference between the student's cost of attendance and the amount the family is expected to contribute to the student's education.

Need Analysis

This process of analyzing the student's financial need assesses how much the family can reasonably be expected to contribute to the student's education, using the family's income, assets and living expenses. The law for federal student aid programs specifies a need analysis formula that produces the Expected Family Contribution (EFC). The postsecondary institution uses the EFC and its own cost of attendance to calculate the student's need and to award grants, campus-based aid and subsidized loans. The college may ask the student to fill out additional forms. This will be in addition to completing and filing the FAFSA. Cost of attendance in this context includes tuition, fees, an allowance for living expenses, books, supplies, miscellaneous expenses and transportation costs.

The Financial Aid Package

The college financial aid administrator uses all available federal, institutional and other aid to build a financial aid package that comes as close as possible to meeting the student's demonstrated financial need. Because of limited funds the financial aid awarded may be less than the amount for which the student is eligible, resulting in a financial gap to be filled by the student's family.

This information reaches the student in the form of a financial aid award letter. If the student's parent feels that the family does not have the means to cover the resulting shortfall, the student may contact the financial aid office of the school to appeal the aid award. This effort may not necessarily result in a more favorable financial aid package. The student and his/her family may wait for financial aid packages from other schools and draw a comparison chart before deciding on which one to accept. As stated earlier, the student may not select the college with the most favorable financial aid package if that college is not high on his/her list of preferred schools for several reasons.

Students need to be aware that in cases where the sum of grants and scholarships they obtain from their communities and other outside agencies exceed their demonstrated need, financial aid offices of colleges may adjust their awards accordingly. This is to enable colleges provide aid to other students in need.

As you plan for the college applications phase of your high school career, you could make the process less stressful by starting early. Allow adequate time for a thorough completion of your applications and essays. Request your teacher and counselor recommendations on time, and work with your parent/guardian and counselor on financial aid and scholarship matters. Be mindful of all deadlines and know that your academic progress must continue. Perhaps thinking of college admission as an important special project will help you greatly with this part of your high school life.

APPENDIX

Source for Chapter 13

U.S. Department of Education, Federal Student Aid, Student Aid Awareness and Applicant Services, *Counselors and Mentors Handbook on Federal Student Aid*, Washington, D.C., 2007.

Some Online Resources

- Testing Information:
  www.act.org
  www.collegeboard.com
- United States Marine Corps: **www. marines.com**
- The U.S. Army: **www.goarmy.com**
- Student Aid on the Web: **www. FederalStudentAid.ed.gov**
- *Funding Education Beyond High School: The Guide to Federal Student Aid*: **www.FederalStudentAid. ed.gov/guide**

- Looking for Student Aid: **www. FederalStudentAid.ed.gov/LSA**
- Fact Sheets: **www.FederalStudentAid.ed.gov/ pubs**
- FAFSA on the Web and Federal School Codes: **www.fafsa.ed.gov**
- FAFSA4CASTER--early estimate of aid eligibility: **www.FederalStudentAid. ed.gov**